CW01082692

Original title:

Towers of Verse

Author: Thor Castlebury

ISBN HARDBACK: 978-9916-88-084-5

ISBN PAPERBACK: 978-9916-88-085-2

Playgrounds for Poets

In the heart of quiet streets,
Whispers dance on fleeting beats.
Dreamers gather, words collide,
In the shadows, thoughts reside.

Language swings on gentle breeze,
Nurtured under ancient trees.
Verses climb like children play,
In this space, they find their way.

Spinning tales on weathered floors,
Imaginations open doors.
Every laugh, a stanza shared,
In the light, their hopes declared.

Ink and laughter intertwine,
In these moments, poets shine.
Each corner holds a story bright,
A playground forged in shared delight.

Celestial Cadence

Stars weave tales in night's embrace,
Whispers of dreams in quiet space.
Galaxies dance in rhythmic flow,
Echoes of love in twilight glow.

Comets trail with fleeting grace,
Illuminating time and place.
Moonlight bathes the silent sea,
Singing soft, a melody.

Heights of Harmony

Mountains rise to kiss the sky,
Windswept whispers passing by.
Echoes of laughter, breezes play,
Nature's symphony on display.

Valleys cradle tales of old,
Stories of warmth in legends told.
In every rustle, a song enfolds,
Life's sweet tapestry unfolds.

Verses Against the Horizon

As the sun dips below the sea,
Colors clash, wild and free.
Painted skies an artist's dream,
Waves of light gently gleam.

Horizons stretch, a vast embrace,
Time stands still, lost in grace.
Every heartbeat feels the pull,
Nature's canvas, beautiful.

The Skyline of Sentiment

High above, the city sighs,
Concrete beauty under skies.
Windows reflect the sunlight's spark,
Dreams take flight, igniting the dark.

Heartbeat of life in every street,
Stories echo, bittersweet.
In the skyline, hopes ascend,
Every moment, a love to lend.

Elevated Expressions

In the heights where dreams reside,
Thoughts collide like stars at night.
Whispers of the heart confide,
In shadows cast by silver light.

Words like feathers gently fall,
Painting skies with vibrant hues.
Echoes of a silent call,
In each stroke, a world we choose.

Lines Reaching Upward

Beneath the vast and endless blue,
Lines stretch forth like eager hands.
Reaching out to fathom true,
The melody that nature bands.

In every twist, a tale is spun,
Of hearts that dare to rise and soar.
Chasing light beneath the sun,
Where dreams take flight forevermore.

Verse Architecture

Each stanza built with care and thought,
A structure bold that stands the test.
With bricks of words, the dreams are wrought,
In harmony, they find their nest.

Foundations strong in rhythm's beat,
A dance of phrases intertwined.
In every line, the heart can meet,
The silent whispers of the mind.

Sonnets in the Sky

Upon the canvas blue and bright,
Sonnets float like clouds afloat.
Verses woven, pure delight,
Each word a softly echoing note.

In twilight's glow, they find their place,
A tapestry of love and lore.
Within the stars, they trace the grace,
Of dreams fulfilled forevermore.

Rhymes Rising

In the dawn, the silence sings,
Whispers capturing gentle things.
Hope and dreams dance in light,
Chasing shadows, taking flight.

Words like rivers softly flow,
Through valleys where the wildflowers grow.
Nature's canvas, vast and grand,
Painting stories, hand in hand.

The Altitudes of Artistry

On mountains high, the eagles soar,
A brush in hand, they seek to explore.
Every stroke, a vision born,
In the light of a new dawn.

Crafted by the heart's own fire,
Art reveals what dreams aspire.
Colors blend in soft embrace,
Creating beauty, finding grace.

Poetic Pinnacles

Where verses meet, the souls align,
In starlit skies, our words entwine.
Each syllable climbs to the peak,
Echoes of the heart we seek.

With every rhyme, a journey starts,
Building bridges between our hearts.
From humble roots, we reach up high,
Touching the canvas of the sky.

Edifices of Emotion

In the chambers where feelings dwell,
Stories woven, time will tell.
Each brick laid with thoughts profound,
An edifice no storm can drown.

Brick by brick, we build and share,
Emotions strong, beyond compare.
From laughter's peak to sorrow's base,
In this structure, we find our place.

Aeries of Artistry

High above in crafted skies,
Brushstrokes dance, the spirit flies.
Colors blend, a subtle call,
Masterpieces rise, breaking the fall.

Whispers of the heart take flight,
In every hue, a spark of light.
Canvas dreams, they intertwine,
In a world where colors shine.

Sanctuaries of Simile

Metaphors bloom like fragrant flowers,
In gardens rich with hidden powers.
Each thought a seed, to gently sow,
In fertile minds, they softly grow.

Echoes of wisdom softly tread,
In quietude, where shadows wed.
Analogies weave through the air,
Binding hearts laid boldly bare.

Bastions of Imagination

In castles built of dreams and light,
Creativity takes its fearless flight.
Walls adorned with visions bright,
Guardians of the deep insight.

Endless realms where wonders play,
Each new thought, a bright array.
Through portals wide, we journey far,
Guided by our inner star.

Vertices of Vision

At the peaks where dreams align,
Perspectives shift, our sights define.
Angles sharp and curves that bend,
In every view, new paths extend.

Focus sharp like an archer's aim,
Charting courses through the game.
With every glance, a world unveiled,
In vertices where hearts have sailed.

Peaks of Poesy

In the dawn where dreams unfold,
The whispers of the brave and bold.
Mountains rise with tales untold,
In the heart, their beauty holds.

Winds weave songs of ancient past,
In every gust, a spell is cast.
Footsteps echo, shadows cast,
On this journey, memories last.

Stars align in night's embrace,
Guiding souls to find their place.
Among the heights, we find our grace,
In peaks of poetry, we face.

Nature's canvas, painted bright,
In every hue, the spirit's light.
With each line, we take to flight,
Above the world, we reach new height.

Columns of Cadence

Amidst the rhythm of the street,
Life dances on in heartbeat.
Each step a pulse, a steady beat,
In columns tall, dreams we greet.

Voices rise in harmony,
Melodies of old and free.
Echoes blend in symphony,
A tapestry of unity.

Through ups and downs, we sway and glide,
With every message, hearts collide.
As time flows on, we walk with pride,
In cadence strong, we shall abide.

Let the music fill the air,
With whispers soft and moments rare.
In columns high, we find our share,
Of life's sweet joy, beyond compare.

Fortresses of Thought

In chambers deep where ideas grow,
Fortresses built, strong and slow.
With every thought, a seed we sow,
In minds of many, wisdom flows.

Walls adorned with dreams and schemes,
Guarding hopes and radiant beams.
Shadows flicker, illuminating dreams,
In fortresses, we find the means.

Battles fought in silence bold,
Stories written, secrets told.
Through trials faced, our spirits hold,
In fortress strong, our heart is gold.

A sanctuary for the wise,
Where insights bloom and visions rise.
In the depths, we realize,
Fortresses of thought, a grand prize.

Skylines of Syntax

Words like buildings touch the sky,
In syntax strong, they soar and fly.
Constructing visions, oh so high,
In literary realms, we try.

Each sentence carved with care and grace,
A skyline formed in paper's space.
With every thought, a new embrace,
In the art of words, we find our place.

Punctuation marks like stars align,
Creating pathways, prose divine.
In every clause, connections twine,
A skyline bright, where dreams combine.

Through verses penned and stanzas drawn,
We shape the dawn, a new day's spawn.
In the brilliance of the endless dawn,
Skylines of syntax carry on.

Inspiration in the Air

A whisper on the breeze,
Ideas take to flight,
They dance in light of day,
Igniting minds so bright.

A spark within us glows,
Creativity unfolds,
In shadows of our dreams,
A story yet untold.

The world, a canvas pure,
With colors vast and wide,
Each stroke a heartbeat strong,
With passion as our guide.

Let thoughts take wings and soar,
Release all doubt and fear,
For in the air we breathe,
Inspiration lingers near.

Peak Prose

Atop a mountain high,
Words gather, clear and bold,
Echoes of the heart's song,
In valleys, tales unfold.

A writer's quest begins,
With ink as rain, it falls,
Each sentence crafted well,
A tapestry enthralls.

With peaks of thought we climb,
In search of greater truth,
Each paragraph, a step,
Reveals the spark of youth.

The summit shines with light,
As stories intertwine,
In prose, we touch the stars,
Crafting dreams, so divine.

Walls of Wisdom

Upon these sturdy walls,
A wealth of tales reside,
Each marking holds a truth,
In whispers, they confide.

The ancient echoes call,
Their lessons clear and wise,
Reflecting on the past,
With every glance, we rise.

In time-worn stones we find,
The roots of who we are,
A bridge to future dreams,
A compass, and a star.

Let wisdom guide our path,
As we embrace the night,
For in these walls resides,
A glow of endless light.

Floating in the Verse

In currents of the words,
We drift on gentle streams,
Each syllable a wave,
A vessel for our dreams.

Through stanzas we will sail,
With rhythms as our guide,
In oceans vast and deep,
We'll never lose our stride.

The poetry we weave,
A tapestry of sound,
In every line we find,
A universe profound.

So let us take the leap,
And plunge into the flow,
For floating in the verse,
Is where true magic grows.

Monoliths of Meaning

In shadows cast by ancient stone,
Whispers linger, softly grown.
Veins of thought through time they weave,
Silent tales that we believe.

Footsteps echo on the ground,
In this silence, truths are found.
Each chiseled mark, a story's thread,
In the stillness, voices spread.

Underneath the starry dome,
These giants speak of time's own tome.
Words unspoken, lives entwined,
In this space, thoughts are aligned.

Rhythmic Ascent

Hearts beat in the pulse of night,
A dance of dreams, a soaring flight.
Each step forward, a melody,
In the glow of destiny.

Breath taken with each new height,
Rhythms flow, guiding light.
Sculpted air, a canvas wide,
On this journey, dreams abide.

Over peaks, the colors blend,
Harmony, the journey's end.
Voices rise, a vibrant sound,
In this climb, we're tightly bound.

The Summit of Expression

With pen in hand, we reach the peak,
Words like rivers start to speak.
Summit high, where thoughts align,
Every line, a sacred sign.

Beneath the vast and open sky,
Ideas soar, they dare to fly.
In the stillness, truth prevails,
Echoes linger, heart exhales.

At this height, all doubts dissolve,
Problems faced, they too evolve.
The view is clear, vision bright,
In expression, we find our light.

Poetic Spires

Rising tall, with grace defined,
Lines of passion, gently twined.
In every verse, a dream takes flight,
Reaching upward, into the light.

Winds of change swirl around,
Carrying whispers through the ground.
Each spire stands, a tale to tell,
In the heart where echoes dwell.

With every stanza, life we trace,
Finding beauty in the space.
Through poetic heights, we explore,
The essence of what we adore.

Echoes of Elevated Dreams

In the quiet whispers of the night,
Stars paint dreams in silver light.
Thoughts take flight, soaring high,
Carried on winds, through the sky.

Shadows dance beneath the moon,
A melody of hope, a gentle tune.
Wishes woven in twilight's seam,
Lost in the echoes of a dream.

Voices murmur in a silent plea,
To grasp what lies beyond the sea.
Mountains bow to those who wish,
As wishes float like a drifting fish.

With every heartbeat, spirits rise,
Chasing fragments of the skies.
In the realm of dreams, we find,
The echoing whispers of the mind.

Sentinels of Stanza

Standing tall, the poets write,
Chronicling dreams in the fading light.
Each word a guardian, fierce and true,
In stanzas that breathe life anew.

Verses march in rhythmic line,
Guarding secrets, aged like wine.
Echoes of thoughts in twilight's embrace,
Sentinels, tracing time and space.

With ink-stained hands and hearts of fire,
They weave the tales that never tire.
In every stanza, a world unfolds,
A tapestry of stories told.

Under skies of endless blue,
The poets craft, and they imbue.
Sentinels watch as verses gleam,
In the heart of every fleeting dream.

Altitudes of Expression

High above in realms of thought,
Words take wings, beautifully sought.
In the clouds, where musings sway,
Art finds its voice, come what may.

Breathless dreams in the azure wide,
Each line a journey, a thrilling ride.
In the heights where silence sings,
The heart discovers what joy brings.

Mountains echo with every rhyme,
Capturing the essence of time.
In the thrill of peak and crest,
Expression finds its truest rest.

So let us climb to lofty vision,
To find in words, our inner mission.
In altitudes where ideas roam,
The heights of expression lead us home.

Citadels of Rhyme

In the fortress where the verses dwell,
Citadels rise, casting a spell.
Brick by brick, the lines construct,
A haven where muses are introduced.

Strong and sturdy, they guard the fire,
Of creativity's unquenchable desire.
Every couplet, a battlement proud,
Standing firm amidst the crowd.

From lofty towers, the voices call,
Wrapped in rhythms, they never fall.
In laughter and in tears, they bind,
The stories of humankind, intertwined.

Within these walls, the heart takes flight,
In citadels gleaming in the night.
Rhyme secures what hearts compose,
A legacy of verses, forever glows.

Verses in the Ether

Whispers float on gentle breeze,
Thoughts like clouds drift with ease,
Echoes of dreams softly call,
In the vast, where shadows fall.

Words unfurl like wings in flight,
Chasing stars in the quiet night,
Each syllable a fleeting spark,
Illuminating the endless dark.

In the silence, stories weave,
A tapestry that we believe,
Boundless tales in every breath,
Life's soft music, defying death.

Let this dance of verses sing,
A serenade from the soul's spring,
In every line, a world anew,
Verses in the ether, always true.

Shelters of Stanzas

In the pages, shadows play,
Guarded dreams, kept at bay,
Each line a storm, a gentle rain,
Finding peace within the pain.

Rhythms pulse like heartbeats near,
Secret whispers only we hear,
Beneath the roofs of words we hide,
A sanctuary, our hearts abide.

Stanzas offer sweet embrace,
Wrapped in tales, a warm space,
As verses shelter fragile thought,
In ink and paper, solace sought.

Here, we find our place to rest,
In written worlds, we are blessed,
Shelters made of dreams and rhyme,
Timeless refuge, transcending time.

Above the Opinion Clouds

In the heights where eagles soar,
Voices soft, they whisper more,
Above the noise, the chatter dims,
In this space where truth begins.

Hearts open wide, like skies at dawn,
Dreams take flight, new paths are drawn,
United thoughts, we rise above,
In harmony, we find our love.

The beauty lies in unseen sights,
Beyond the struggles, the petty fights,
In this realm, perspectives shift,
Life's canvas bright, a precious gift.

With every breath, we build and grow,
Above the clouds, the answers flow,
In shared beliefs, we find the gold,
A brighter future, brave and bold.

The Rhythm of Heights

Mountains hum a steady beat,
Nature's heart, a syncopated feat,
In the heights where silence sings,
We dance beneath the wide spread wings.

Echoes bounce off stone and air,
Life's pulse felt everywhere,
In every step, a voice of grace,
Finding joy in this sacred space.

Skies stretch wide, the sun does reign,
Chasing clouds through sunlit rain,
In every moment, we are free,
Dancing to our own decree.

With every drop, a note we find,
In nature's arms, we unwind,
The rhythm of heights, a timeless song,
Together, we know where we belong.

Aerial Arrangements

Up high where breezes play,
The clouds drift in a dance,
Colors blend and softly sway,
In nature's grand expanse.

Kites that flutter, soar, and glide,
Whisper dreams on gentle winds,
They chase the sun, no need to hide,
As bright new day begins.

Birds compose a fleeting song,
Notes that echo from the skies,
Harmony where they belong,
Painting blue with joyful cries.

In this realm, the heart takes flight,
Where gravity feels less defined,
A canvas vast, pure and bright,
A space where souls unwind.

Celestial Constructions

Stars above, they twinkle clear,
A patchwork of forgotten dreams,
Galaxies that beckon near,
In the dark, a thousand gleams.

Planets spin in cosmic dance,
They weave their tales in cosmic light,
Each orbit holds a fleeting chance,
To glimpse the infinite night.

Nebulas in colors bold,
Paint the heavens rich and bright,
Stories waiting to be told,
In the vast, enchanting night.

Wonders born from stardust's grace,
In each shimmer, hope's embrace,
A universe, both vast and small,
Reminding us, we're part of all.

Verse Cascades

Words like water gently flow,
In rhythm soft, they wend and weave,
Crafting tales from ebb and glow,
Whispers, secrets left to cleave.

Each line a ripple, pure and clear,
From pools of thought they leap and glide,
In every stanza, echoes near,
Like memories caught in the tide.

Pages turn, the journey sings,
In currents deep of prose and rhyme,
Connecting hearts through written strings,
A dance that bridges space and time.

Let your spirit dive within,
Embrace the flow of written grace,
For every verse where dreams begin,
Is a cascade we can trace.

The Summit of Rhyme

Atop the hill where words align,
The peaks of thought rise high and steep,
In every hue, a word divine,
Awake the muse from slumber deep.

Echoes of poets long ago,
Whisper secrets on the breeze,
In every stroke, the heart can grow,
Finding solace, moments freeze.

Climb each line, one step at a time,
Discover worlds wrapped in each phrase,
With every rhythm, every rhyme,
You'll find the sun of inspiration blaze.

Reach for the sky, let verses chime,
In the climb, we share our truth,
For in the summit of pure rhyme,
Lies the boundless spirit of youth.

A Canopy of Words

Beneath the leaves, whispers float,
Secrets held in gentle note.
Each word a petal, soft and bright,
In the silence, they take flight.

Stories tangled in twisting vines,
Innocent laughter, soft designs.
Words like rain, they dance and play,
A canopy where dreams can stay.

Sunset glimmers in golden hues,
Painting tales of love and blues.
The breeze carries the tales afar,
A symphony beneath the star.

In this grove, let hearts be free,
Under the shade of memory.
Each whisper shared, a wild bloom,
In the word's embrace, find room.

The Skyline of Soliloquy

In the stillness, echoes soar,
Thoughts like clouds, they gently pour.
Voices rise to greet the dawn,
In solitude, new dreams are drawn.

High above, the stars align,
Guiding hearts through curves divine.
Each murmur, a bridge to the sky,
Connecting souls that pass by.

In the dusk, reflections gleam,
Painting visions, kindred dreams.
Whispers weave through night's embrace,
In shadows, find a sacred space.

Let the skyline hold our breath,
In the silence, we conquer death.
With every thought, take to flight,
A soliloquy in the night.

Ramps of Reflection

Steps ascend on gentle ground,
In quiet thoughts, peace is found.
Each ramp a journey, winding slow,
Carving paths where waters flow.

Mirrors gleam in twilight's call,
Reflecting moments, one and all.
In stillness, echoes softly break,
Revealing truths that shadows make.

The spirit lifts on each new height,
Harnessing day and cradling night.
With every glance, a story spins,
Ramps of reflection, where life begins.

Step by step, feel the grace,
In the climb, we find our place.
Embrace the light on every rise,
In the journey, wisdom lies.

The Height of Harmony

In unity's embrace, we stand tall,
A symphony that encompasses all.
Every note, a vibrant thread,
Woven gently, where love is spread.

Chords entwined as seasons shift,
Harmonies in nature's gift.
A dance of voices, pure and bright,
Echoes that spring to life at night.

In the height where dreams converge,
Melodies and visions surge.
Together we find sacred ground,
In the chorus, joy resounds.

Let each heart beat in time,
To the rhythm, sweetest rhyme.
In this height, forever soar,
In harmony, we are much more.

Heights of the Heart

In whispers soft, the heart does soar,
A longing that can't help but implore.
The skies above with colors bright,
Lead dreams to dance, like stars at night.

In valleys deep, where shadows play,
The echoes of love find their way.
Through every trial, each tear's release,
We find the strength, and moments of peace.

With every heartbeat, a tale unfolds,
Of love that's rich, and never cold.
Through highs and lows, we climb the part,
To reach the heights of the heart.

Empyreans of Eloquence

Words like angels gracefully glide,
Through thoughts and dreams, they swiftly ride.
Each syllable a spark of light,
Illuminating the dark of night.

In realms where silence often reigns,
Eloquence flows, release from chains.
With every phrase, a story born,
In the dawn of language, we are reborn.

A symphony of voices soar,
Echoing wisdom from ages yore.
In every whisper, a secret gleams,
In the empyreans of our dreams.

Verses in Skylines

Skylines brush against the blue,
A canvas bright, where dreams come true.
With every tower that scrapes the sky,
A testament to hopes that fly.

In the twilight glow, shadows twine,
Drawing patterns, sweet and fine.
Every window, a story's show,
Tales of love, of loss, of woe.

Underneath the city's heart,
Life unfolds, a dynamic art.
In every corner, whispers blend,
Verses in skylines never end.

Grids of Rhyme

In grids of rhyme, the patterns weave,
Each line a gift, a tale to leave.
Words intertwine in playful dance,
Creating worlds, a vivid expanse.

With stanzas set, and rhythms drawn,
The heart of poetry carries on.
Each couplet's form, a gentle guide,
In the mosaic of the mind, they bide.

From chaos springs a structured grace,
In every stanza, a sacred space.
As verses bloom and thoughts align,
We find our truth in grids of rhyme.

Canopies of Creativity

Beneath the leaves of vivid hue,
Ideas flutter, born anew.
Whispers dance in twilight's glow,
Painting dreams where thoughts can flow.

Branches sway with gentle grace,
Inviting minds to find their place.
A tapestry of bold design,
In every corner, visions shine.

The sky above, a canvas bare,
Fills with colors beyond compare.
Each brushstroke tells a secret tale,
In this realm where wonders sail.

Under canopies, we dare to dream,
Unraveling the threads of a vibrant theme.
Creativity blooms in the tranquil air,
Nurtured by the love we share.

Cliffs of Contemplation

Standing tall on rugged stone,
Thoughts run deep, but we're not alone.
Wind whispers secrets lost in time,
Encouraging hearts to ponder and rhyme.

Edging close to the vast unknown,
Where waves crash in a rhythmic tone.
Each echo a question, each spray a thought,
In the silence, answers are sought.

Shadows dance as daylight wanes,
Illuminating all our pains.
Atop the cliffs, we find our voice,
In stillness, we make our choice.

With each sunset, wisdom grows,
Guiding us where the river flows.
As stars emerge, we breathe, we trust,
In contemplation, all is just.

Platforms of Passion

Rising high, the hearts unite,
On platforms bathed in golden light.
Voices soar, both loud and clear,
In the space where dreams appear.

A stage of hope, bold and bright,
Ignites the flame within the night.
Each heartbeat echoes, a timeless beat,
Passion pulses, strong and sweet.

Hands together, we stand as one,
Together igniting, brighter than the sun.
In every breath, a story shared,
The fire within, unafraid and bared.

With every leap, we chase the stars,
No matter how distant, no matter the scars.
Platforms of passion, we rise and fly,
Embracing the dreams that never die.

Ascendancy of Allegory

In tales spun with threads of gold,
Allegories of the brave and bold.
Each story whispers wisdom deep,
In shadows where the secrets sleep.

Mountains climb, and rivers bend,
Every twist brings a new friend.
Symbols dance upon the page,
Unraveling truths, wisdom's sage.

Through trials faced and lessons learned,\nThe fire of
hope forever burned.
Each parable a step we take,
In search of meaning for our sake.

Ascending high, we seek the light,
In allegory, day turns to night.
With every echo, the mind set free,
In stories told, we find our key.

Pyramids of Prose

In the sands, stories rise,
Layered words touch the skies.
Whispers of ancient might,
Crafting shadows in the light.

Brick by brick, tales unfold,
In the warmth of gold and bold.
Sculpted thoughts, a sight to see,
Building dreams, setting them free.

High Grounds of Imagination

On the peaks where visions soar,
Mind's eye opens, craves for more.
Clouds are curtains, dreams are plays,
In this realm, the spirit stays.

Casting shadows on the ground,
Where ideas spin round and round.
Above the world, the heart can breathe,
In a plot where dreams believe.

Stanzas Against the Skyline

Verses tower, bold and true,
Against the sky, a vibrant hue.
Words like wings take to flight,
Painting stars with ink and light.

Every line, a bridge to roam,
Echoing in the heart, a home.
Stirring souls with gentle grace,
In this verse, we find our place.

Eloquent Elevation

In the heights where echoes ring,
Every whisper, a song to sing.
Words ascend, a dance of thought,
In the silence, magic's sought.

Each syllable, a step we take,
Through the clouds, our dreams awake.
Reaching peaks where we belong,
In the heart of the written song.

Pillars of Poetry

In the quiet night they stand,
Whispers of dreams in soft command.
Words like bricks, stacked so tall,
Each line a promise, never to fall.

Crafting worlds with ink and thought,
Every verse a battle fought.
Foundations firm, they won't decay,
Holding stories in their sway.

Heartbeats echo, rhythms chime,
Shaping moments, bending time.
Through the silence, voices sing,
In the shadows, hopes take wing.

Pillars of truth, of love's embrace,
In the heart, they find their place.
Let the verses rise and soar,
In the realm of poetry, forevermore.

Stanzas Ascending

Each stanza a step, a climb so steep,
Words take form, and visions leap.
Reaching for heights, where dreams reside,
In valleys of thought, we dare to glide.

Ascending mountains of crafted light,
Each phrase a spark, igniting the night.
With every line that lifts the soul,
We find the depth, we find the whole.

Ink spills like streams, pure and bright,
A dance of language ignites the night.
Hearts in sync, we rise as one,
In this journey, there's no done.

Stanzas growing towards the sky,
In this rhythm, let us fly.
Together we weave our tales of old,
In the tapestry of words, brave and bold.

Echoes of Heights

In the mountains, whispers call,
Echoes of tales, where shadows fall.
Voices carry on the breeze,
Making memories with such ease.

Each peak a story, high above,
In every verse, we find our love.
Resonating through the air,
In echoes, we find solace there.

Nature's song, in harmony,
With every line, we feel so free.
Scripted dreams in heights we reach,
Lessons in the silence teach.

Echoes linger, soft and clear,
A reminder that we hold dear.
With every word that finds its flight,
We touch the stars, we claim the night.

Versified Peaks

Climbing steep, we find our way,
Verses guide us, come what may.
Every syllable, a foothold found,
In the landscape of thoughts profound.

Peaks of meaning rise and fall,
In the silence, we hear the call.
Crafting dreams with every breath,
In the poetry, we dance with death.

The view is clear from heights we reach,
Each line a lesson, none to teach.
On this journey, we hold each hand,
Together, we make our stand.

Versified peaks, where voices blend,
In this moment, we transcend.
With every word, a passion sparked,
In the world of verses, we are marked.

Climbing Through Cadence

Steps that echo in the air,
A rhythm found up high,
Breathless moments fill the space,
Where dreams begin to fly.

Each stone a story left behind,
With whispers from the past,
We climb the notes of nature's song,
In harmony, we're cast.

Horizon calls with vibrant hues,
The summit's sweet embrace,
In every beat, the heart aligns,
With time and sacred grace.

Above the clouds, the world unfolds,
A tapestry of light,
We find our rhythm, bold and free,
In this transcendent height.

Verses Among the Vistas

Waves of green stretch far and wide,
A canvas brushed by dreams,
In every valley, stories sleep,
Among the flowing streams.

Mountains rise like ancient kings,
Guardians of the tales,
With every shadow, every dawn,
The compass never fails.

The sun drips gold on winding paths,
As whispers guide the way,
In verses rich and full of life,
We wander, lost in play.

Among the vistas, hearts collide,
In silence and in sound,
Each moment crafted, piece by piece,
In nature's beauty found.

Nests of Narratives

In branches high, a tale takes flight,
A nest of whispered dreams,
Stories woven, fine and bright,
In sunlight's golden beams.

The chirps of morning break the calm,
Awakening the earth,
Each flutter speaks of life's sweet song,
Of love and endless worth.

Beneath the leaves, a history,
Protected from the storm,
In nature's arms, we find our place,
And feel our spirits warm.

These nests remind us, soft and true,
That every heart belongs,
In tales of joy, in threads of blue,
We join the world's grand songs.

Rhymes in the Ether

In whispers soft, the verses dance,
Like shadows in the night,
Each word a spark, a fleeting chance,
To capture pure delight.

Clouds above, they cradle thoughts,
A symphony of dreams,
In every breath, a story wrought,
In moonlit silver beams.

The stars align, like notes in time,
As echoes drift away,
We find the rhymes in endless space,
Where night becomes the day.

In all the wonders yet to come,
The ether sings its song,
Each heartbeat paints the world anew,
In rhythm, we belong.

Pinnacles of Poetic Wonder

Above the clouds, where dreams reside,
Words dance freely, side by side.
In whispers soft, the muses sing,
Igniting hearts with every swing.

Through valleys deep, the echoes flow,
Crafting tales of joy and woe.
Nature paints a vibrant scene,
In colors bold, a world unseen.

With each breath, a story spun,
Beneath the moon, beneath the sun.
Eternal flames of passion bright,
Ignite the soul, illuminate the night.

From peaks of thought, to depths of sound,
In every heart, true love is found.
These pinnacles, a timeless flight,
In poetic wonder, pure delight.

Heights of Harmony

In tranquil skies, the melodies soar,
A symphony of life, forevermore.
With every note, our spirits rise,
A dance of dreams beneath the skies.

Each heartbeat syncs with nature's tune,
Painting warmth beneath the moon.
A gentle breeze, a whispered grace,
In harmony, we find our place.

Together we stand, hand in hand,
Creating a world we understand.
From mountains high to rivers wide,
In heights of harmony, we abide.

Through every storm, we find our way,
The sun will shine, come what may.
In unity, we bloom and grow,
Heights of harmony, love's pure glow.

Structures of Soliloquy

In quiet moments, thoughts arise,
Whispers echo, a world of sighs.
Within the mind, a labyrinth spins,
Exploring depths, where silence begins.

Each structure built with care and grace,
Reflections cast on time and space.
Words entwined in thoughtful threads,
In soliloquy, the spirit spreads.

Beneath the weight of quiet fears,
We unearth the laughter, tears.
In solitude, the truth unfolds,
A tapestry of stories told.

In every chamber, light will play,
Illuminating shadows gray.
Structures of soliloquy speak,
In hushed tones, the heart will seek.

Spires of Sonnet

Reaching high, the spires gleam,
Anchored deep in a timeless dream.
In verses crafted, love takes flight,
A sonnet's heart, both bold and bright.

Each line a step, each rhyme a bridge,
Connecting souls, our hearts, a ridge.
Through starlit nights and golden days,
The spires stand in poetic praise.

With passion poured in every word,
A symphony of love unheard.
In every sonnet, truth reveals,
The deeper essence that love feels.

As twilight falls and shadows creep,
In whispered lines, our secrets keep.
Spires of sonnet, high and grand,
In poetry's embrace, we stand.

An Arch of Imagination

Beneath the sky so wide and vast,
Dreams weave tales that hold us fast.
Colors dance in mind's embrace,
Each whisper paints a wondrous space.

In shadows deep where visions play,
Thoughts ignite then fade away.
With every breath, new paths unfurl,
A tapestry of a vibrant world.

Stars flicker bright like scattered dreams,
In silence spun, with gentle seams.
Imagination lifts us high,
On wings of thought, we learn to fly.

Through arches formed of purest light,
We chase the dawn, we greet the night.
In every heart, a spark resides,
That leads us on where freedom glides.

The Pinnacle of Poeticity

Atop the hill where silence sings,
Words take flight on unseen wings.
They swirl and dance like autumn leaves,
In every whisper, magic weaves.

Starlit skies, a canvas bright,
Each line a brushstroke of pure light.
Born from dreams, they find their way,
To touch the soul, to softly sway.

The heart awake, with pen in hand,
Creates a world where spirits stand.
In every verse, a heartbeat flows,
A tale of life, it gently shows.

In twilight's glow, the muses speak,
Of love and loss, of strong and weak.
The pinnacle awaits the brave,
For in their words, the world we save.

Elevated Epics

In realms where heroes find their quest,
Stories rise to conquer the rest.
With courage bold and hearts ablaze,
They carve their paths through shadows' haze.

Each battle won, each tear that falls,
Echoes heard in ancient halls.
With swords of truth and shields of grace,
They face the trials that time will trace.

Mountains tall and rivers wide,
They journey forth with strength and pride.
Through haunted woods and skies of grey,
They seek the light to guide their way.

As tales unfold and legends grow,
In every heart, the embers glow.
For in each epic, life is drawn,
A song of dusk, a hymn at dawn.

Celestial Chronicles

In the stillness of the night,
Stars converge in shared delight.
Each twinkle sings a tale of old,
Of cosmic dreams and truths untold.

Planets spin in rhythmic grace,
Tracing paths in endless space.
Galaxies swirl in timeless dance,
Inviting souls to take a chance.

Constellations weave a lore,
Of love and loss, of seas and shore.
With every glance at skies above,
We find the threads of boundless love.

In celestial scripts, our hearts reside,
Among the worlds, we turn the tide.
For in the universe's embrace,
We pen our stories, find our place.

Structures of Sound

Whispers dance in twilight air,
Echoes caught in shadows fair.
Rhythms weave like threads of gold,
Stories in their silence told.

Notes that flutter, soft and bright,
Fill the dark with pure delight.
Harmonies that blend and sway,
Lift our hearts, then drift away.

In the void, a symphony,
Carried forth with reverie.
Beats that pulse beneath the skin,
In each moment, life begins.

Structures built from sound and air,
Crafting worlds beyond compare.
Melodies that swirl and rise,
Painting beauty in the skies.

Verses in the Clouds

Drifting thoughts in azure blue,
Words like feathers, light and new.
Stories born in skies above,
Whispered there with gentle love.

Puffy shapes that roam the day,
In their shadows, we can play.
Verses float on breezes mild,
Nature's breath, both wise and wild.

Each cloud holds a verse or line,
Woven dreams, a grand design.
In the dusk, their colors blend,
A soft tale that has no end.

Verses born from whispered sighs,
Mingle with the fading skies.
In their realm, our thoughts take flight,
Chasing dusk and welcoming night.

Poetic Frameworks

Lines awaken, strong and true,
Like a bridge from me to you.
Stanzas rise, a crafted art,
Echoes of the human heart.

Every word, a step we take,
Forming paths that we will make.
Verses anchor thoughts so deep,
In the silence, we will leap.

Rhythms guide the hands that write,
Carving visions into light.
Metaphors that blaze and burn,
Teach us all we have to learn.

In the end, we find our ways,
Within the framework of our days.
Each poem holds a truth so bright,
A beacon shining in the night.

Lyrical Heights

Reaching high, the verses soar,
Touching dreams we can't ignore.
With each line, we climb the skies,
Finding beauty in our cries.

Words that dance on zephyr's breath,
Celebrate both life and death.
In the mountains of our mind,
New horizons we will find.

A symphony of thoughts untold,
Adventures waiting to unfold.
Lyrical heights, a vast expanse,
Inviting all to share the dance.

Together we will rise and sing,
Embracing what the heavens bring.
In harmony, our spirits gleam,
Charting forth each sacred dream.

The Dance of Lines

In shadows cast by twilight's glow,
Lines intertwine, a gentle flow.
They sway like whispers in the night,
A ballet soft, a dream in flight.

With every curve and every bend,
The dance of lines knows no end.
They echo secrets, tales untold,
In a canvas bright, their grace unfolds.

A stroke of ink, a spirited roar,
Across the page, they seek to soar.
They twirl through space, embrace the air,
A symphony crafted with flair.

So let them dance, let colors blend,
In this sweet art, our souls transcend.
For in each line, a story sways,
The dance of life forever plays.

Echoed Aspirations

In the heart where dreams collide,
Whispers of hope shall reside.
A voice that carries through the air,
Echoed aspirations everywhere.

Each longing finds its way to light,
Guided by the stars so bright.
In every wish, a passion burns,
A cycle of life, as the world turns.

We chase the echoes of our past,
In every moment, shadows cast.
With every step, we pave the way,
To brighter futures, day by day.

Let dreams resound, let spirits fly,
In the vastness of the sky.
For every voice in harmony,
Creates a world where we are free.

Lyrics Among the Stars

In the silence of the night,
Stars compose a tune so bright.
Each twinkle tells a tale of old,
Lyrics whispered, dreams unfold.

The cosmos sings in vibrant hues,
A melody for hearts to choose.
In the vast expanse, we find our place,
In every note, a warm embrace.

So let us dance beneath this sky,
As constellations drift on high.
With every breath, the universe flows,
In the symphony, our spirit grows.

In cosmic realms, our voices rise,
The lyrics soft as lullabies.
Together we create the spark,
That lights the path within the dark.

Sublime Structures

Amidst the chaos, forms arise,
Sublime structures grace the skies.
In harmony, they stand so tall,
A testament to dreams that call.

Each corner holds a whispered thought,
In every beam, a battle fought.
Geometry of life and space,
In every line, a sacred place.

With pillars strong and arches wide,
A journey starts, a place to bide.
In every wall, a story lives,
Of all the moments that it gives.

From simple roots to grand design,
Sublime structures intertwine.
Together they create our past,
A future built to ever last.

Foundations of Metaphor

In shadows deep, truths intertwine,
Words hold worlds, gently defined.
A bridge of thought, unseen yet clear,
Emotions dance, drawing us near.

Layers of meaning, rich and vast,
Colors of language, shadows cast.
A whispered tale, a silent shout,
In every phrase, a hidden route.

Crafting dreams from whispered sighs,
A canvas stretched beneath the skies.
Foundations strong, yet light as air,
In every metaphor, we share.

With every turn, a new surprise,
A tapestry of truth that flies.
In the heart of words, we come to see,
The endless depths of poetry.

Monuments of Muse

In quiet corners, inspiration waits,
Chiseling thoughts, opening gates.
Monuments rise, bold and grand,
Crafted softly by a steady hand.

Echoes of passion in stone and time,
Verses unbound, a rhythm, a rhyme.
From whispered dreams to concrete form,
A sculptor's heart, forever warm.

Each statue tells a silent tale,
Of hopes and wishes that cannot pale.
Muse in the shadows, guiding the way,
Creating wonders, day by day.

With brush and pen, we shape the sky,
In the gallery of thoughts that fly.
Monuments stand, a legacy true,
Reflecting the beauty found in you.

Bulwarks of Balladry

In tales of old, where echoes blend,
Ballads rise, and hearts extend.
Each verse a shield, each line a wall,
Guarding dreams, they stand tall.

Rhythms rumble like thunder's sound,
In melodies lost, true strength is found.
Echoing voices from ages past,
Binding the future with shadows cast.

From whispered lore to epic fights,
Each story shared ignites the nights.
Bulwarks strong, of joy and sorrow,
Shielding the hopes of tomorrow.

In every song, a journey starts,
Uniting souls, connecting hearts.
The power of ballads, forever ours,
Anchored in life, like ancient stars.

Ascents of Alliteration

In a world where words entwine,
Syllables soar, with grace they shine.
Climbing high on rhythmic waves,
Alliteration, a dance that saves.

Silent whispers bring forth delight,
Fluttering phrases, taking flight.
From gentle sounds to bold, bright calls,
The magic of language in grand halls.

With every step, the verses gleam,
Crafting wonders, like a dream.
Ascents of sound, they twist and turn,
In every heartbeat, lessons learned.

Echoing laughter, a playful tease,
Words like feathers, carried on breeze.
In the melodic spell we weave,
Alliteration helps us believe.

Living Lines in the Wind

Whispers dance on the gentle breeze,
Thoughts entwined in the rustling leaves.
Stories told through the swaying grass,
Time unfolds in each moment that passes.

Dreams take flight on the winding paths,
Hope found where the horizon laughs.
Each breath carries a tune so bright,
Living lines in the fading light.

Nature's script flows like a river wide,
In every shadow, secrets abide.
Windswept tales of the world entwined,
Echoes of life through the open mind.

The heart beats strong as the winds will sway,
A symphony sung in a vibrant display.
In every breeze, a new refrain,
Living lines in the wind remain.

Lingering Lyrics Above

Stars twinkle softly in the velvet night,
Their songs linger on, a delicate flight.
Whispers of dreams in the moon's embrace,
Floating gently in the cosmic space.

Clouds drift slowly, a canvas bright,
Painting the skies with colors of light.
Each note a memory, softly spun,
Lingering lyrics, where stories begun.

Constellations sing of ages past,
Fables of love in the twilight cast.
Melodies woven through time and air,
In the silence, a connection rare.

Lifted spirits, beneath starlit glow,
Hearts unite in the rhythm we know.
In dreams we soar, forever free,
Lingering lyrics, a sweet harmony.

Elevated Euphony

Melodies rise like the morning sun,
Graceful notes in a dance begun.
Harmony flows through valleys and hills,
Echoes of joy, where the heart fulfills.

Voices entwined in a chorus bright,
Lifting souls to the boundless height.
Each sound a promise, each tune a spark,
Elevated euphony in the dark.

Rhythms weave through the fabric of days,
Turning simple moments into a blaze.
Cascading dreams like a waterfall's light,
In every heartbeat, the world feels right.

Symphonies linger in the gentle air,
Filling the silence with love and care.
Together we rise in the music's embrace,
Elevated euphony, a sacred space.

Infinity in Ink

Words flow freely like rivers of thought,
Captured moments in pages sought.
Ink spills stories, both old and new,
Infinity rests in the lines we drew.

Characters dance on the stage of dreams,
Life's intricate web, unraveling seams.
Each letter whispers secrets to share,
Infinity in ink, beyond compare.

Ink-stained fingers, a heart laid bare,
Pages turning with a tender care.
Thoughts etched deeply on the canvas wide,
In every word, a world resides.

Stories unbound, in time's embrace,
In the written word, we find our place.
Threaded together, our lives inked true,
Infinity in ink, forever anew.

Lofty Lines and Lifelines

In skies so vast, where dreams take flight,
The lofty lines converge with light.
We chase the stars, we reach for more,
Each lifeline drawn, a whispered score.

Beneath the clouds, our hopes entwine,
In every breath, the heart's design.
Through storms we sail, with spirits high,
These lines connect us, you and I.

With every step, we write our fate,
In lofty heights, we contemplate.
The horizon glows, a guiding flame,
Together forged, we build our name.

So let us rise with every dawn,
In symphony, our souls are drawn.
These lofty lines within our grasp,
Create a future we embrace, clasped.

Ridges of Reflection

Upon the ridges where silence dwells,
The echo of thoughts in whispers tells.
Each valley deep, each peak we climb,
Reflects the shadows, lost in time.

In nature's arms, the spirit finds,
A solace deep, where truth unwinds.
The rustling leaves, a gentle sigh,
Call us to linger, to ask why.

As twilight fades, the stars emerge,
In quiet moments, our hearts surge.
With every glance, a story we earn,
On ridges high, for wisdom's turn.

So stay awhile, let shadows play,
In reflection's grip, we find our way.
Within the stillness, life unfurls,
Among the ridges, a dance of twirls.

Nebulae of Narration

In cosmic clouds where stories weave,
Nebulae glow, long tales conceive.
Stars born anew, their paths ignite,
Each twinkle holds a world in sight.

Through swirling dust, our voices soar,
In distant realms, we yearn for more.
With each creation, a journey spun,
A tapestry rich, under the sun.

As night unfolds, the galaxies speak,
In whispers soft, they find the weak.
Nebulae of dreams, forever bright,
Guide us through the endless night.

So let us gaze, and share our lore,
In every heart, the cosmos pour.
With stars aligned, our fates combine,
In nebulae's glow, our stories shine.

Outposts of Observation

Atop the hills, the outposts stand,
With watchful eyes, we seek the land.
Each sunset paints the world anew,
In observation, we find our view.

Through whispered winds, the secrets flow,
And in the stillness, truths will grow.
The horizon calls, our hearts inclined,
To see what lies beyond the blind.

With every breath, the moments freeze,
In nature's hands, we find our peace.
At outposts high, our spirits meet,
In silent vows, our dreams complete.

So let us stand, and seek the stars,
In every glance, erase the scars.
The outposts weave a sacred thread,
In observation, our souls are fed.

Words in the Wind

Whispers dance through the trees,
Carried softly on the breeze.
Echoes of stories, long untold,
In the silence, they unfold.

Every leaf a tale to share,
Secrets spun in the open air.
Nature speaks, its voice a guide,
In every gust, dreams collide.

Footsteps trace the paths of thought,
In the stillness, wisdom's sought.
Listen closely, hear it blend,
A symphony that will not end.

Words like feathers, light and free,
Drifting through eternity.
Embrace the song, let it flow,
In the wind, true stories grow.

Heights of Reflection

Mountains rise, their peaks in sight,
Skyward visions, pure delight.
In the stillness, thoughts emerge,
Atop the heights, spirits surge.

Clouds like whispers passing by,
Moments captured in the sky.
Silent echoes of the past,
Reflections deep, shadows cast.

Glimmers of hope in every glance,
In the heights, we take our chance.
Soulful views in quiet grace,
Finding peace in nature's space.

Beneath the stars, we pause and dream,
In this realm, no need to scheme.
High above, the heart takes flight,
In the silence, we find light.

The Language of Loftiness

In realms where eagles dare to soar,
Words find wings, forevermore.
A dialect of dreams untamed,
In lofty heights, we feel unclaimed.

Conversations with the sky,
Meaning bursts, like stars on high.
Breathless moments, thoughts align,
Poetic echoes, sharp and fine.

Let the clouds be your retreat,
In the sublime, we find our beat.
Every sigh a verse of grace,
In the sky, our hearts embrace.

Language flows like rivers wide,
In this vastness, hearts abide.
Embrace the words, let them spin,
In every breath, the world begins.

Summit of the Soul

Climbing high, we seek the peak,
Insights stir, profound yet meek.
Every step a story told,
In the summit, hearts turn bold.

Gazing down at paths we've passed,
Moments fleeting, shadows cast.
Silent prayers upon the stone,
In this stillness, we are known.

Wisdom whispers to the brave,
In the heights, we rise and wave.
Embracing silence, finding peace,
At the summit, doubts release.

Here we stand, the world below,
In the heights, our spirits glow.
Every breath, a tribute made,
In the soul's own serenade.

Poetic Peaks of Thought

In valleys deep where whispers dwell,
The mountains rise, their stories tell.
Each peak a thought, a flight of dreams,
In silent hearts, we craft our schemes.

Through shadows cast by fading light,
We seek the heights, embracing night.
With every step, a voice will call,
To lift us high, to never fall.

A canvas vast, the sky in hue,
Paints hopes anew in shades of blue.
Each star a wish, a guiding spark,
Illuminating paths through dark.

So let us climb, with joyful glee,
To peaks of thought, where we are free.
For in the heights, our spirits soar,
Found in the dreams we can't ignore.

Heights of Passion

In hearts ablaze, the fire ignites,
A dance of souls on starry nights.
With every glance, a spark will fly,
Our passion burns, it cannot die.

We chase the dawn, our spirits bold,
In whispered vows, our truths unfold.
With every kiss, the world is still,
In heights of love, we climb at will.

Like rivers flow, our hearts entwine,
In every moment, your hand in mine.
Together we rise, hand in hand,
To heights of passion, a promised land.

So let the stars bear witness now,
To love that breathes, to hearts that vow.
In every heartbeat, life's sweet art,
We find our strength, we find our start.

Ethereal Expressions

Through moonlit dreams, our thoughts take flight,
In whispers soft, we share the night.
With colors bright, our feelings blend,
In ethereal strokes, we transcend.

Each fleeting moment, a canvas clear,
Expressing truths we hold so dear.
In swirling hues, emotions flow,
A dance of light, a vibrant show.

With every sigh, a story spun,
In timeless echoes, we become one.
The brush of fate paints paths divine,
In ethereal expressions, we shine.

So let us wander, hearts laid bare,
To seek the beauty, to find the rare.
For in each stroke, our spirit guides,
In dreams that linger, love abides.

Towers of Thought

In silent minds, the towers grow,
Built from the dreams we dare to know.
Each brick a wish, each beam a hope,
In towers of thought, we learn to cope.

They pierce the sky, a vision clear,
Reaching for heights, we hold most dear.
With every word, they rise anew,
A testament to all we pursue.

In shadows tall, we seek the light,
To scale the walls of day and night.
With courage bold, we face our fears,
In towers of thought, we shed our tears.

So let us build, with heart and mind,
These structures vast, for all mankind.
For in the thoughts that tower high,
We find our strength, we learn to fly.

Milton Keynes UK
Ingram Content Group UK Ltd.
UKHW031412131024
449461UK00006B/38